daydreams
and deliriums

Reflections of a Mediocre Mind

Ramesh Thampi

For those who live in self-doubt,
every other day;
including *you*…

#1
2016

Time flows, sluggish and wavering,
like the footsteps of a drunkard.

My girl, do not cry—
for I was just a leaf, carried away by the wind,
fallen on to your lap for a fleeting moment of love…

#2

2017

I had surpassed a few moments of despair—

Against the flow, against the norms,

Against the fleeting glares of insanity,

And the unforgiving heralds of insane morality.

I had surpassed a few moments of passion too—

When her little murmurs soothed my heart,

When her steamy breaths tingled my neck;

She was a wild horse, who refused to be tamed,

But for those brief moments when I did,

She took me through the best rides of my life.

I had surpassed a few moments of glory—

When the claps raised to rumble the roofs of vanity,

When praises were precious than anything,

And time flew like a wind of storm.

I had surpassed a few moments of envy too—
The worst of all, the deepest scathing blade,
Piercing through skin and reason
All the way to our wounded naked souls;
When your brother gets the better half of the cake,
When your close friend gets a quickie with your crush;
When the world moves forward while you stand still,
When your dreams are lived by someone else.

I had surpassed a fair share of them all,
And gave my inner demons a good fight to sing;
Like you, like your ancestors,
Like your bleeding soul that leaves back a trail of stains.

#3

2016

There is only one way,

To survive in this boring world—

With a burning passion,

To something,

To anything,

Even folly or non-sense.

Bukowski said:

"Find what you love and let it kill you."

You are going to die anyway—

Bored to death!

#4

2016

What do you want?
She asked.

To become immortal,
And then die.

#5

2016

All I want in life is—

a false sense of purpose,

even to do the menial daily tasks…

A grandiose meaning—

intertwining past and future

to the present.

A revelation—

while pretending to meditate,

amid overflowing thoughts.

An omen—

while I casually spit on a calm lake,

creating ripples of consequences.

An insight—

when the drizzles hurt my face,

while I gaze out of a moving bus.

An inspiration—

while watching movies, reading books,

resounding with my current state of needs.

All I want in life is—

cling on to my self-image,

even while the earth implodes…

Consider how lucky I am

to have friends on social media…

Believe how special I am

even if no one notices my sudden demise…

Show off as if my life's awesome,

even while I'm just fooling around *online.*

And convince myself somehow—

that one day,

I'm going to make it to the grave.

#6

2016

I was that insignificant howl of a night creature,
taking one moment of attention from those around;
but, that was enough—
to keep me alive,
to keep me away from my tormenting loneliness…

#7

2019

In a lifetime,

when time flies by

and slows down,

the only time I feel *less* insane

is while I'm all alone,

resting on your lap,

underneath a billion shimmering stars.

#8

2016

When I look at my bookshelf

and bury my face on those aging papers,

inhaling their intoxicating seductive odors,

I am reminded of—

the stories behind obtaining those,

the people who gifted them,

a nostalgic period in my life,

a bookstore from which I shoplifted,

the memories of a girl with a halo behind her head—

altogether,

teleporting me into a land of broken nostalgic dreams…

They say,

a picture is worth a thousand words;

but,

a picture remains the same to thousands,

while a hundred words

instill zillion meanings in a single reader.

#9

2019

Why is it that,

good times feel good

only when it's over;

but, bad times feel bad,

even while we are in it?

#10

2016

Oh, my dear Multiverse,

save me from this dilemma of sorts,

for I am just another random soul,

wasting my time, trying to figure out—

the meanings behind my ever-changing realms of
thoughts…

#11

2016

Yearning for a tale untold to anyone before,

I strayed through the woods, searching for the story-teller;

The one who whispers fairy-tales to sleeping writers,

Since time unknown, for ages beyond.

While I stared at the empty sheets,

She ignored my prayers, my calls for Muses;

As if blessing someone else

In another corner of the dark wide world.

I walked again,

Passing the shadows of a jungle so deep,

Crawling through its entangling branches,

Seamless intertwined sagas of fortune and grief.

Getting lost,

Stopping each time to marvel

At her magic shows and spectacles,

Creations of grandeur and ordinariness,

Journeys and fables of epic love,

Adventures and struggles for power,

Sorrows and tragic nuances,

Resistance of the oppressed,

Cities burnt and rebuilt,

Wars fought for freedom and women alike,

Lives un-lived and gold mines un-earthed,

Greatness and insignificance,

You and me.

Yearning for a tale untold to anyone before,

I waded forward through the slippery paths;

Passing caves of mysterious mythic charm,

Reptiles slithering across with a funny laugh,

Dragons appearing to be slain through battles,

And rabbits digging holes and inviting me over...

When I saw her, knitting threads of narratives,

A gentle breeze passed by,

Chilling currents surging through my spine;

With tingling eyes,

When I felt my fingers over the fabrics,

The time got frozen, and a moment was captured;

In a flash of lightning,

She raised her hand and slapped me real hard,

Shaking me up from a very deep slumber...

#12

2016

I used to dance under the rain;

And then,

I bought a Smartphone.

#13

2016

How many of you still believe,

you're destined to do something amazing,

rather than just creep through the day-to-day obligations,

infotainment addiction,

and the mere acceptance of everything as it may come?

#14

2017

And when the sun sets,

I know my days are ending too;

Flabbergasted by the haze of it,

And the boredom that snatched away the gist of it.

In my days of naivety,

I was a better man still—

For I fought with all my heart,

My scars oozing bloods of passion.

In my days of future,

I see sparkles of timidity—

Permeating through my sutures,

And gripping me with a fear of mortality.

#15

2016

Under our armors we hide,
Not knowing, its weight is dragging us behind;
Not knowing, the blows aren't hard as we think.

If you're living the same day over and over again,
Once in a while—drop the defense and keep the doors
open,
For new winds may take you to unknown places.

When sunlight filters through the pine-forests,
Melting boundless fields of snow,
You'll know for once, you were right in taking the
journey.

Always asked myself the question—
'What's the point of being alive?'
And while wandering around, seeking something,
The mountain breeze whispered the answer.

#16

2016

You might want to

put a dent in the Universe;

but,

all I want is—

put a tent on mountain-tops.

#17

2019

Mountains do not talk;

They listen intently,

With their stone-age hardened souls.

A sudden whoosh of wind, rustling prayer-flags,

A few withering leaves, a spark of snowfall,

A play of mist and fog, or a gentle fall of rocks…

That's how they cry—

For those leaving them behind,

For us wandering minds—

Anticipating our seemingly endless comebacks.

#18

2016

Travelers are lone spirits,

escapists,

living in the wrong spaces.

They suffer with heaves of ancestral guilt,

when stuck for long in their native places,

shattered by monotone routines of familiar pastures;

They sit idle, but their minds wander off,

for the only way to reclaim their lives—

is to move forward anyway, no matter what.

With the last breath of strength left,

I would sneak away too—

In search of souls on similar wave-thoughts,

Into the voyages of miles afar…

#19

2015

When eyes and minds

Shift from one screen to another,

Once in a while,

I turn nostalgic—

About the ancient rains,

Catching tiny fishes with towels,

Dropping them on water-filled coconut husks,

And shifting them to glass bottles,

Where they live and mate

for the rest of their lives.

#20

2014

What we had lost is that cool sense of *wonder*,

Simple practical methods to overcome a problem,

The joy of *sharing* the excitement,

The *courage* to get out there and get what we want,

And not letting our *spirits* down by what others think or say...

#21

2016

Dear Shah Jahan,

When I stand before the magnum opus,

I don't judge you;

I just wonder

If I,

Or anyone since you,

Could ever create a better symbol,

For our love towards someone alive even.

#22

2016

There is no particular meaning,

or purpose,

for our existences;

You are born with the liberty,

to create

to choose

to assign

or

to imagine—

the meanings you want.

#23

2016

Of all the dreams I had ever seen,

Searching for you remains my favorite—

Through the last rains of the season,

And the first fall of the snow;

Through the scorching heat on barren valleys,

And shape-shifting sand dunes with unforeseen storms;

Through narrow mountain passes with deep gorges aside,

And hanging bridges with roaring rivers beneath;

Of all the dreams I had ever seen,

never I lost sense of reality before—

Straying away from running crowds,

From one town to another of odd survivals;

Bearing the heaviness of my empty soul,

Along the nothingness that lay until the horizons;

Of all the dreams I had ever seen,

never I had been so desperate before...

In search of you, I walk the downtrodden paths again—

To meet with you, to share stories with your listening heart,

To stargaze together, and to finally let you know—

You are not just another random soul…

Of all the dreams I had ever seen,

never once before I desired not to wake up again….

#24

2012

They say,

The reason you can't sleep at night is—

you're in someone else's dream.

Tell me,

Who's dreaming about me regularly?

Who's behind my constant nocturnal insomnia?

#25

2017

Tired,

of fighting all the wrong battles.

Exhausted,

of loving all the wrong women,

and men.

#26

2015

Even today,

When I hold that old lined notebook of poems

—About our little talks,

Stolen moments,

Secret glances,

Shivering touches,

And gentle kisses—

Close to my chest,

I can still hear,

The fluctuating rhythms of your beating heart.

#27

2017

Isn't it better,

to

Leave with regret,

than,

to

Live with regret?

#28

2016

My backpack is a treasure bag,

filled with

empty diaries,

broken fountain pens,

unread books,

unposted letters,

unrequited love,

and unrealized dreams.

Forgive me dear,

for my only disease,

the worst of all,

is half-heartedness.

#29

2018

Unconditional love

is

an

amateur's

favorite

fantasy.

#30

2016

Have your hands ever shivered,

while unwrapping a gift-cover,

and holding a new book,

fresh in its enticing fragrance,

so fresh that you want to postpone reading

for a few more days?

#31

2017

In order to be free,

You have to tie yourself down,

And see how far you can endure.

You have to understand the contradictory viewpoints,

Forget what you saw and understood,

And unlearn to learn yet again…

In and out of a pre-designed, pre-caricatured lifestyle,

All you fear of is falling par below it;

But,

All I fear of is—

Being constrained within its virtual boundaries,

Or the real limits of our spirits and bodies.

#32

2015

I miss that kid—

His wonder, for those river-shore shells,

His energy, that built castles of sand,

His spirit, that climbed trees and conquered,

And his mindless runs after moons and birds.

Then there was fire,

Search for the new,

From ashes, from libraries,

From pixels of porn.

The frets, the sudden tantrums,

The cries for acceptance,

The inability to accept oneself;

The hot sun, the damn heat,

The dust, the rush, and the crowd;

The crowd within—

Complaints, desires, blames,

Mental chatters, melancholic memories,

And the longing for miracles.

And now, bitten by egos and ideas,

Injected by dead doctrines,

Religion, political endeavors,

Fights against the rights of others,

Voyeurism, repressed sexualities,

The search for love and hope…

And tomorrow,

The marrow-tickling fears—

of turning insignificant,

being forgotten,

vanishing all of a sudden,

like stardust shot into the void of space.

#33

2012

I'm the captain of the pirates—

My future chained under the shacks,

Riding on the turbulent black seas,

Fighting the storms, charming the tides,

Finding heavenly islands all through the way…

#34

2016

Experiences are prerequisites,

not the goals—

said the interviewer,

to a frustrated job-hunter.

#35

2019

Have your ever forgotten yourself,

in your mindless scrolling to the endless depths of your

social media feeds?

Have you ever considered yourself as an explorer,

lost in the exotic worlds of your latest video games?

Have your ever loathed yourself,

jerking off to the acrobatics of others,

playing in multiple tabs of your browsers?

Have you ever wondered why you never belong

to your little world of average people,

doing mediocre jobs?

Have you always believed,

that internet will save you no matter what?

Have you considered asking other people of your age,

whether their feelings are similar to yours,

to find out that you are neither unique nor original?

#36

2013

Those weren't morning dews,
But tears of the flowers…

#37

2016

Insignificant

One in billions

Wandering around

On the road

Off the tracks

Scribbling stuff

Hanging to memories

Offering help

Snatching guilt

Loving too much

Hating much more…

Yet feeling too special

In my own mindless thoughts…

#38

2014

I want to live in an uninhabited island,

Where flowers bloom and birds sing,

Where love is not yet forbidden…

I want to live in the present,

Sleep while asleep, aware while awake;

And meet a lost girl from my dreams,

Make intense love under the stars,

And create a lost generation together…

But now,

I dream while asleep,

I dream while awake,

And I dream about making love all the time…

#39

2018

Your passion lies in—

Wanting to create,

With *something* you constantly think of;

You know,

You constantly think of nothing but Sex—

Nature's default programming

To make you create more miserable copies of yours.

#40

2014

The secret of existence,

the way of nature,

is simple—

Fragrant flowers could become

stinking filth,

and vice versa!

#41

2019

An idea in itself is a parasite,
In need of hosts, to draw blood from,
And thrive in repeat-mode—
Like *Ophiocordyceps unilateralis.*

And extremists are like *zombie ants*—
Driven by something other than themselves,
To stab, kill, attack, or turn to suicide bombers,
All for their fairy-tales and fictional ideologies…!!

#42

2019

Once upon a time,

have you written exams with fountain pens,

shaking out drops of ink on the wooden desk,

then sucking it up using nibs,

and continue writing with enhanced clarity,

or repeat the process,

just to pass the time

until the bell rings once again?

#43

2019

I want to die a 72-years old hopeless lover,

My memories lost in oblivion—

Yet remembering a seven-digits landline number,

That does not exist anymore!

#44
2019

A tourist follows a rigid plan—

Sight-seeing upon pre-written itineraries,

Window-shopping every other souvenir,

Dream-walking like a controlled puppet,

And not getting anywhere near the soul of anything.

A tourist runs, while a wanderer walks—

Witnessing the flow of world,

Unhurried to reach any destination,

Unbothered by fears of missing out,

Unassuming about her collection of visa stamps…

Don't be a tourist, be a nomad—

Follow the hippie-trails like a wayfarer,

Trek on ice and conquer your fears like a mountaineer,

Saunter through the unknown terrains like a trailblazer,

And quench your wanderlust by roaming around like a vagabond.

Let your soul get smashed to smithereens

and bury those pieces in different places

and go back one day to see if they had sprout and grown…

Don't be a tourist, be a voyager,

be a seeker of your own multi-dimensional possibilities…

#45

2019

I want to spend the nights,

Smoking pipes,

Sipping a glass of vintage red wine,

Listening to Frank Sinatra on vinyl records;

Cutting out photos and articles from newspapers,

Going through my collections of stamps and comics,

Writing letters with an antique feather quill,

And creating prose on a Smith-Corona typewriter;

Dial my land phone to invite a friend over,

And debate in cafés, drinking tons of black coffee…

Hopping from one bar to another in a Parisian street,

Gulping whiskies, hugging strangers, seducing
waitresses,

Singing out loud poetries until the emergence of dawn…

I want to spend my days and nights

In another world, in another era,

In the lost memories of writers and poets and artists…

#46

2019

We are the middle-children,

crammed between

the old-school and the quick rise of technology…

We are the last generation,

to play home-building as kids,

with sticks and leaves,

with mud and rocks.

We are the last generation,

to have listened to music in cassette-tapes,

Struggling to put back the tape,

when it got jammed in players.

We are the last generation,

who felt horny by reading porno-magazines,

switching to video cassettes, CDs, DVDs,

computers, pen-drives, internet, laptops,

phones, Bluetooth, SD cards, slow-speed downloads,

smart phones, tablets, and even Virtual Reality...

We are the connecting link,

the lost generation,

the Millennials,

the *'neither here nor there'* ones...

#47
2015

Reality
is
just
a
shared
dream.

#48

2016

Somewhere,

Two lovers had a pillow-fight;

Someone carried a bag,

Collecting those cotton memories flying around....

Somewhere,

On the darkest hours,

Someone brought some light;

The sleepers woke up, blaming him...

Somewhere,

Someone killed a mosquito

And cried for long;

It was her own blood.

Somewhere,

On a full moon night,

Someone went looking for

Dancing naked pagans.

Somewhere,

Someone puked some random hollow borrowed words,

Posed as insight.

~   ~   ~   ~   ~   ~   ~

Printed in Great Britain
by Amazon

33195782R00040